When Miracles Aren't Enough: The Lessons Tragedy Taught Me

When Miracles Aren't Enough: The Lessons Tragedy Taught Me

❖

By Erica Kosal, PhD

With contributions from Braxton and Annalise Young
as well as Brian Etheridge

Illustrations by Annalise Young

Burro Publishing

When Miracles Aren't Enough
By Erica Kosal
Published by Burro Publishing
www.bouncetoresilience.com
Copyright © 2016 Burro Publishing

For information, contact the author at erica.kosal@gmail.com
Library of Congress Cataloging-in-Publication Data Pending

ISBN: 978-0-9856809-2-3
E-book ISBN: 978-0-9856809-3-0

Editor: Gail M. Kearns, www.topressandbeyond.com
Book and cover design: Robert Aulicino, www.aulicinodesign.com

Printed in the United States of America

TABLE OF CONTENTS

To Patty Aune, a true friend, and all the family and friends that helped me get through the hard times, showing me that love and goodness still exist in the world

To my children, Braxton Young and Annalise Young, two amazing people that are a constant blessing in my life

And as always
To Jim Young, my sweet husband, who was a bright light in this life and whose wisdom and kindness helped make me the person I am today

INTRODUCTION

My husband Jim was only fifty-six years old when he died. Our children were only seven and five on that late June day when Jim was with us in our home for the last time. His decline and our battle, however, started years prior. In fact, it all started during a time when our son, the oldest child, was learning to walk. When our second child, our daughter, was born, Jim started heavy medication and treatment for neurological chronic Lyme disease. He was already struggling so much, but determined as ever, we chose to focus on the good and believed that his illness was temporary. We could handle the hell that was present in our life knowing that sometime in the near future Jim would be well again. He would be whole, and our dreams and the life we had envisioned could continue.

During that November of 2008 when our daughter Annalise was born, Jim and I thought we were in the worst of it. We figured that Jim was so weak and so drained there was no way it could get worse. We reasoned that if we could make it through the next several months of heavy IV antibiotic treatment and massive fatigue, muscle cramps, sinus headaches that wouldn't go away, and juggling work with letting the body heal, we would be alright. Jim was a hard worker. Jim was meticulous and on top of his illness. Jim was persistent and able to suffer through some awful months with a smile on his face the whole time. The promise of restoration was on the horizon.

If anyone could do it, we knew it would be Jim.

But things were not alright. Six years later, with periods of recovery followed by downward dips in health, Jim was in and out of the hospital several times for weeks at a time. He had a tracheostomy and, at first, was on a ventilator for several hours at night, but eventually Jim required twenty-four-hour assistance breathing. Jim had a feeding tube inserted. He had embolisms, several episodes of his lungs collapsing, epiglottis issues, swelling over his entire body such that he was hardly recognizable as himself, and a host of other awful things that ultimately resulted in Jim being unable to walk or move without assistance. On top of this, to add insult to injury, over the years, it became more and more difficult to talk and communicate with Jim. At first, I could read his lips, but as the years passed, Jim had a harder time enunciating his words, and, in turn, I had trouble deciphering them. Initially, Jim could move his hands to spell letters, and I could figure out the words quickly—oftentimes before he finished spelling the complete word—and so a conversation could flow easily enough. But then his hands didn't want to work; the muscles had atrophied too much. Jim then turned to using a pointer. He could hold it in his hand with assistance and indicate letters on a letter board. Eventually that became too difficult as well.

To say it was tough watching someone I loved go through this is an understatement. In fact, it is impossible to communicate the emotions that became part of my existence. It was especially tricky to get a grasp of them because our children needed a fully present mother. At times I felt like a ping-pong ball going from one emotion to the other. I was strong for Jim, an advocate for his health needs. I was "on" for the kids and trying to keep things very family-friendly for us all. We managed to do many things as a family—going to school functions, seeing movies, attending soccer games—but there were many times that I functioned as a single mom, shuttling the kids here and there, making major decisions on my own, fretting over finances, cooking dinners while working full-time and taking care of my husband, and trying desperately to do some "typical" activities and have times for the kids to be kids.

When Jim's health started to decline many years prior to his death, we spoke at length about several things. Among them, the two things that were most important to us were that we manage things as best as we could so that the kids would have as normal a childhood experience as we could provide, and additionally, that we strive to find the good in this mess. We knew there must be something of value that we could gain from the experience. In the spirit of this latter goal, and upon reflection of my journey through Jim's illness and death, I decided to write this book.

As I reflected on things I learned, I realized there were several. I also realized there were serious things I knew already that had been tucked away and neglected in my mind. There were those "my mother used to tell me when I was little" reminders, but there were also those "yep, no wonder there is that expression" reminders, too. I have chosen to write about these insights in no particular order. I have also chosen to include some insights that I blogged about over the years so that you can gain some insight into our lives, as well as share some beautiful thoughts from my children.

I will not understand the why to all of this while still alive myself, but I have faith that there is good to take from my experience. If I focus on the contribution and impact that Jim has had on our friends, family, and even strangers who have reached out to us, good can be found. Jim was a giving and kind soul who inspired many people both during his healthy years and again during his sick years. Jim's life mattered, and many people have witnessed the good that his life brought forth, including our children and me.

Blog Entry, May 28, 2014 (about a month before Jim died): The Gentleman's Birthday

My husband's birthday is here—I wasn't sure he would make it this year. He continues to decline, in bed, unable to move and breathe on his own, and he sleeps about nineteen hours a day. What kind of celebration can we have? My typical question I ask at birthdays, "What are your goals for next year?" seemed illogical. I don't know how much time is left for Jim's next year.

Coupled with a celebration is the idea of a birthday gift. I like the tradition of acknowledging the value of the person on his birthday, but what specific gift could I offer my husband on his birthday this year? I have been trying over the past several months to give Jim a sense of how much he is loved and how much he inspires by creating a CD with his favorite songs and collecting stories about him from friends and family. But still, a birthday should be specifically celebrated. Always. It is the day Jim came into the world. It is the day that someone who has influenced so much and so many should be acknowledged. And so, with this in mind, I decided to focus on the one word I have used so many times to describe Jim—gentleman—and the legacy which that offers to our two children.

What does it mean to be a gentleman today? The word seems old-fashioned in many ways, but also distinguished and honorable. When many of us think about a gentleman, we think about someone who holds open doors for people, who takes the time to say hello to everyone, and who may dress in a certain classic way. We may also think about a person who is duty-bound, respectful, and someone who finds value in tradition. This is Jim, but his gentleman ways are broader than this.

When I looked up the word in the dictionary, this is what I found: "a man who treats people in a proper and polite way." There are two things that strike me about this definition. The first is the verb "treat" and the second is the adjective "proper." This is different from what I described above—related, but still different. Notice the verb itself is treat. Treat. It is not a state of being as we often associate with the term gentleman, but rather an action. To treat people a certain way. My husband Jim has always been one to treat others with respect. It didn't matter who the person was—how old she was, how he dressed, what words came out of their mouths—Jim treated every person with whom he came in contact kindly. You might argue he treated everyone properly. When it comes down to it, treating others as you would like to be treated is the proper thing to do. There really shouldn't be anything special about this, yet there is a special word gentleman that we associate with the act of treating others properly.

My suggestion of the term gentleman to describe my husband over the years has spanned from this proper treatment of all, but it was more than this. Jim not only treated the people whom he interacted with well, he went out of his way to engage people who were strangers. He yearned for that connection. He made sure that a person knew she was special. He made sure that his little gestures had a big impact. Jim's gentleman ways also crossed into the aspiration category. By living as a gentleman, he showed others what a life of honor looked like. He showed us all what a better world we could create, if only we all behaved more like gentlemen.

And so, as I teach our children the lessons that I know Jim would be teaching them if he could, I remind them about the big things: "respect people, respect property," and I teach them that small things matter too, such as "hold the door open for everyone coming behind you" and "the man or the adult walks on the outside of the sidewalk" and "you shake a hand firmly, smile, and always look people in the eyes." I hope this gift of passing along Jim's gentleman ways to our children is one that Jim knows is the best gift he has given to us all.

Lesson #1

Focus Your Attention on the Good

As mentioned before, it's a wonderful thing that there is always something of value present in any situation, regardless of how awful it is. I am not naïve enough to think that in the moment of tragedy, if you look at the right place or at the right angle, you will see that diamond sparkling. No, indeed, often during tragedy the good is delayed. However, it does take discipline on one's part to actively seek the good and be present with it. Sometimes there is a period of time in which grief, anger, frustration, and exhaustion are demanded. In fact, these emotions are healthy and necessary. If we focused always on the green pastures over the brown mud, we would be doing our psyche a disservice. In order to validate our feelings and to reflect on the emotions and potential value to be found within these emotions, it's important to realize that things are not good. That times are hard. That the situation is not fair. But it is equally important to actively decide to refocus our attention on a healthier path. At some point, it becomes vital to shake off the mud and all the yuck that is clinging to it and move to another road we have chosen. It will not be the original yellow brick road we envisioned, but it will be one that we have decided on for ourselves, and that can make all the difference in the world.

1

Over the years, rather than let myself sink into depression, I would call a friend. Instead of thinking about Jim's illness, I would focus on the progress he made. Instead of watching a depressing show on TV, I would switch to reading an inspiring true story or listen to a podcast that spoke of good things, promises, and being a light in the world. In general, I actively chose hope. I learned quickly that I did not want to be surrounded by the message of despair, death, and depression. Where I shifted my behavior was mostly with my choice of radio selections. Since my commute to work is one hour in length, I often listened to news radio stations and occasionally talk radio stations for a little variety. I grew to resent the bad news. The constant worry. The ever-present gloom. So instead, I began to listen to inspirational books on CD, to motivational speakers, and to inspiring SIRIUS radio shows. I wanted to hear about success and be reminded that people can overcome and find meaning in the sadness of events.

It quickly became clear that this shift could put my mind at ease, remind me of perspective, and focus my thoughts down a productive pathway. Jim and I had an expression about the devil getting after us when we would start to think sad, awful thoughts. At first this expression was in jest and good-natured. Over time, I realized the truth in the expression. If we didn't shake those feelings away and take the power back ourselves, the devil would in fact win.

It became, and continues to remain, something that I consciously have to do everyday. I pause more than I used to, I reflect more than I used to, and I acknowledge and thank more than I used to. Little things. The beautiful moon. The cut flowers someone dropped off at my door. The laughter of my children. The good that is present.

Throughout the day, constantly and often, seek the good wholeheartedly. In this way, your mind is where it should be and you can aspire to be the kind of person you want to become. It is a process, an evolution, but one that is worth it.

Blog Entry, October 20, 2013:
The Bee Sting Philosophy of Life

It happened the other afternoon. The injustice. The betrayal. The perspective change.

My kids and I were having lunch outside on the patio of a restaurant. It was a lovely October afternoon in North Carolina. The sun was shining and bees were flying about as we ate our sandwiches. This scene was perfect—blue skies, warm temperatures, and insect life surrounding us. The bees didn't bother us; I had taught my kids to be calm around them. I ensured them that the insects were not interested in us and only would sting if we acted crazy, causing the animals to move into defense mode. So there we were, eating, laughing, enjoying the sun, when suddenly I hear my four-year-old daughter screaming like I've never heard her scream before.

Bolting into action, I spun around looking for the culprit. My daughter grabbed her arm and insisted a bee stung her. I couldn't believe it! How was that possible? We followed the rules. The bees crossed the line. Our first reminder that life is not fair.

I quickly picked up my daughter and hugged, kissed, and rocked her as she screamed bloody murder into my ears. But then the pain subsided a bit, and the screaming changed to sobs. After a few more moments, the crying was interrupted by some pauses, and then we moved into recovery mode. Going into the restaurant, I asked for some ice and told the manager what had happened. He looked at me strangely and said, "She is handling the sting very well." She was. I was proud of her. Then he added, "What did you do or say to her that she is so calm?"

"I whispered to her it was not fair that the bee stung her, but that it happened and she needed to decide how she was going to respond to it. It was all up to her."

My daughter has heard me preach this message before. The act itself, and the pain that followed, was not deserved. She did nothing "wrong," and still she was attacked. She could have cried and cried and let her whole day be ruined or she could decide to consider her next moves, play and enjoy the day while letting her body heal itself and focus on that which was still good.

My children hear these words often from me. They have also seen this message play out in our home. Their daddy is so sick, with Lyme disease and ALS-mimic symptoms, he can't talk with them, play with them, or interact with them as we would all like. He did nothing wrong and certainly does not deserve the pain and sadness that accompanies a horrible disease. But he can choose—and by default his family can choose—to look at the good things in life over his bad condition. The event may not be changeable, but how we move on from the event is all ours. I call it The Bee Sting Philosophy of Life.

LESSON #2

PAY ATTENTION TO WHAT PEOPLE DO, NOT WHAT THEY SAY

❖

My mother conveyed these words to me ever since I can remember. Other people have heard the variation: actions speak louder than words. This latter expression was so commonplace at times during my childhood (it was recited by teachers, parents, and coaches), it got to the point that I didn't really hear it. Like a too familiar song playing on the radio, we sing the words and know the times to inflect, pause, and belt out the tune, but we haven't really paused long enough to absorb the meaning of the lyrics. My own mom's version of this came from her mother too. That's how these things go, isn't it? We keep what we learn, what we know, what becomes important. We pass it on, we hope the lesson is learned, and we pray the tradition continues. My family's version is, "Don't pay attention to what people say, look at what they do. This is what is important."

People, and painfully so often friends and family, will say the right things but will not follow through. Sometimes a phrase, a conversation, or a promise is made with good intentions, but time has a habit of moving quickly, and days turn into weeks, and then before we know it, the calendar needs to be turned to a new month. Sometimes words are said out of awkwardness—a person sees we are in pain, sees us suffering, and says something in

5

the hopes of cheering us. Sometimes words are said, just as those memorized popular songs on the radio, out of habit because they are words that are supposed to be said during such stressful, sad times.

These are the worst kind of words. They are hollow and, ultimately, they make us feel abandoned and lonely. They can especially sting if we don't recognize them initially as the trite type of phrases that they are. I have found this to be the case most often when the conversation is coming from someone unsuspecting – for example, a family member who, of course, should care. She says the right things at the right time, seems most troubled by the happenings of the sad moments, but when push comes to shove, she is nowhere to be found.

When Jim first began to get sick, I was so blindsided by these bait-and-switch scenarios that it was almost comical. How many times can I be fooled? I wondered often during those first several years. I was so hurt, but mostly hurt for Jim. I couldn't understand how a loved one could so conveniently not be present or available wholeheartedly for a man who was so kind and giving during his healthy years. I couldn't understand how, over the years, decisions were made to avoid him, and yet these same people had plenty of time to do other things—things that were obviously more important to them but made no sense in the grand scheme of things.

At first, I was unbelievably stunned, then angry, and finally the sadness came. Sadness primarily for Jim, because some of the people we thought would be there weren't. Sadness also for these same people, because in my heart I knew that one day they would likely look back at the events and see the lost opportunities to have spent time with Jim, to have made the trip to sit with him and tell him stories, to learn directly from Jim's words and actions (when Jim was still able to communicate), and to express their love to him.

Fortunately, we had the opposite experience as well. People I never would have expected to be so kind to us showed us love and support time and time again. My first taste of this occurred shortly after Jim had his tracheostomy. It was a very scary time with Jim being rushed to the emergency room, his oxygen levels plummeting, and then the extra-long stay in the hospital. Close friends were tending to the kids, and one of my sisters had flown in to help out as well. After one particularly long day at the hospital, I returned home to find a neighbor sitting on the floor with my son who was then about three years old. She was playing trains with him. Braxton was perfectly content listening to my neighbor. He was engaged and being taught two valuable lessons: people can do nice things for others, and good can be found in any situation. As my neighbor Melanie smiled a big smile, I was struck by the surreal nature of the scene. Melanie was a lovely person but not someone I saw often and not a close friend at the time. She was not someone I would have expected to be at the house. For that matter, I wasn't even sure how she found out about Jim being in the hospital. Melanie's true character continued to shine over the next months and years as she welcomed my children into her home, helped shuttle them to daycare and school, and regularly did things for us without me even realizing that her help was so needed.

There are many other examples I can include that have a similar tone to them: A neighbor, an acquaintance, a friend who I wouldn't have expected to bend over backwards for my family but chose to do so. A neighbor showing up at the hospital with a card, a dozen cookies, and constant prayers. An acquaintance sending a book (*Jesus Calling* by Sara Young) at the precise moment I needed it. Friends who planted pansies in the front flowerbed to remind us we were loved. Neighbors stopping by to trim trees, shovel a snowy driveway, and bring food. The consistency of these acts did not go unnoticed. At times they spoke some kind words, but they never said, "Please let me know how I can help." Instead, they instinctively knew that I couldn't function on that level during this time of stress and tragedy. I couldn't tell anyone what I needed help with because I had no clue. I was in survivor mode. The true friend was the one who called and said, "I'm coming to watch the kids for you for three hours so you can pay your bills," or the friends who came to walk the dog everyday so my energy could be invested in tending to Jim and the kids.

The reminder that actions are more telling than words became clear over my journey; however, my surprise came when people who were not on my radar as supporters turned out to be just that. As for the close friends and family who disappointed? I have tried not to judge, and I acknowledge that everyone handles grief in different ways. I have taken away a new appreciation for the complexity of the human spirit and continue to focus on the good that is present in all situations.

Blog Entry, March 27, 2013:
The Paused Word, the Longer Hug, and the Unspoken Nods

You can tell much about what a person is thinking if you study their body language and facial expressions. Without saying any words at all, if you pay attention to the subtle clues a person is giving, you can determine a lot. It is hard sometimes to make sense of it all, and often there may be a missed opportunity to say something of significance, but the unsaid and the gestures can go a long ways to forge an understanding between two people.

My major experience with this has been found in interacting with my husband. With chronic Lyme disease that has hit his neurological and muscular systems in a fashion similar to ALS, it is currently difficult for him to speak. Even pointing to letters on a board in order to spell out a word can be problematic for Jim, and so I have learned to guess, predict, and try to talk about things in a way that is more story-like in nature rather than discussion based.

The other day I had an experience that I have certainly had before, but it was somehow more powerful this time around— different in some way. One of Jim's cousins and a dear friend came for a short visit. It meant a lot to us because he and his wife live overseas now, and when they do come to the States, they have lots of people to see. When the cousin left, we gave a glance to each other that brought tears to my eyes. The nod that followed from the cousin told me, "I know. This sucks. Hang in there." The bang of that moment was intense. Jolting myself out of it, I hugged his wife, and when I turned to the cousin, I started to say something but stopped. I don't even remember what it was. I paused. He knew I was in deep thought mode and sensed my pause was necessary. Then he waited until we had the exchange of nods again. I was about to walk away, drawing support from my two young children who were playing in the yard, when the cousin leaned in to give me a hug. I thanked him for visiting and hugged him back, ready to say, "Be safe guys. I hope you have a good rest of your visit." But I found myself unable to pull back. The cousin squeezed me again, a little harder and for a few seconds longer, and by doing so gave me such a strong sense of relief that someone got it; things were alright. Not good, but alright. The hug was a reminder to hold on, stay strong, and keep up the fight. People were around my family showing support and love, and they would be there to give a hug or a nod when the time was again necessary.

LESSON #3

THERE IS REAL POWER IN WORDS

❖

The saying "Sticks and stones may break my bones, but names will never hurt me" is just wrong. I know the intention of the expression is to help children focus their attention away from ugly words thrown at them. There is benefit and truth in that. But if a child is convinced that names and words really do not have the power to sway, move, direct, and alter their own behaviors and future events, then the expression may have harmful effects.

Words do matter. Words spoken and words thought. They influence our perception of things. They influence our attitudes. They influence our behavior. They set in motion ideas, attitudes, and behaviors that will impact our and others ideas, attitudes, and behaviors.

Let's take for example how someone views an event and what words she chooses to use to frame that event. Pick anything negative that has happened to you and try to remember what specific words you used when you were conveying the story to a friend or family member. The words you chose influenced how the friend viewed the event, which in turn influenced the words that came out of her mouth back to you, which in turn, of course, influenced your thoughts, feelings, and next set of behaviors.

When Jim first got his correct diagnosis of neurological chronic Lyme disease, it took us a while to come to terms with the illness and what it meant. Because Jim had a lot of symptoms that aligned with ALS (better known as Lou Gehrig's disease), we were in a scary place. But once it came time to tell our friends and family what was happening, we were careful with our selection of words. I remember having lunch with two friends. We met occasionally for birthday lunches and connected over our small sons being in preschool together. "As you guys know, Jim has been struggling with his health lately," I began. They both stared at me in anticipation of what I was going to drop on them. "Well," I continued, "it turns out that we finally have some answers, although there is much that still doesn't make sense to us." I wavered a little in my explanation, wondering if I should fluff it and spin it as a disease that others acquire and beat, knowing that we started our battle late and with Jim's severe symptoms not really matching the more typical Lyme disease victim. My hesitation was momentary. "Jim has late-stage Lyme disease. We don't fully understand what it all means yet, but we have a positive attitude about things. Jim is strong and willing to fight for his health. We know how one views illness goes a long way and that who you surround yourselves with can make or break a person in such a case." I gulped and looked at my friends. These two women were my test subjects. They stared back at me, trying to digest my words. Most people did early on. Jim was young, very healthy up to his point, took good care of himself, and did not look sick. A few more moments passed. I could feel myself squirm in my seat, thinking maybe I had shared too much information. Should I have just said, "Jim's alright but still struggling a bit?" I glanced back in anticipation. They looked at one another, and then one said, "Wow Erica, you guys have the best attitude about this that I've ever seen." A hug and a warm, genuine smile followed. You know, those smiles that only friends can give. My other friend followed suit. "Yes, Erica. Jim is strong. He is determined. If anyone can do this, he can."

Those words held me for years. Time and time again when I started to feel depressed, defeated, or deflated, I would remind myself that Jim was a fighter. He was determined. He could do this. I would tell Jim these things, too. We knew them to be true, and they continued to give both of us the extra burst of energy that we needed to handle another crisis, deal with another logistical paperwork nightmare from the insurance company, see the sun coming up on the horizon, and know that things would be better soon enough.

There is power in words:

"Death and life are in the power of the tongue, and those who love it will eat its fruits." Proverbs 18: 21

A reminder that what we say matters. We can lift people up (ourselves included) with our words, and we can destroy with them as well. We must be prepared to accept the consequences of our word choices.

Blog Entry, March 27, 2013:
The Pleasant List

I went to dinner the other night with two girlfriends. The experience in and of itself was pleasant. Due to all the craziness in my life currently, I don't get out very often. My husband is very ill with chronic Lyme disease and is currently on short-term disability. These days he is having trouble breathing, walking, and interacting with his family. He has a tracheostomy and a feeding tube. Life is not the same as it was prior to the illness, but we are making it work, and my husband is getting stronger slowly but surely. Still, the idea of going out on the town for an evening is usually not on my radar.

Although we have much help from wonderful family and friends during the day, and nurses coming during the night shift, I still work full-time, and I'm raising two children. I have a lot on my plate. Feeling like I am constantly moving at one hundred miles per hour from one thing to another, without much time to digest and think about things, it really was a pleasure arriving at the restaurant to two smiling faces, a glass of wine, and the ability to eat a satisfying "adult" dinner without sweet children trying to sit on my lap, or trying to out-do one another in order to gain my attention by talking in what we call their outside voices.

It was during this dinner that one of my friends was honoring the passing of one of her friends and coworker. Her friend was far too young to have died from cancer, but it was evident this person had a lasting impact on her friends and family. As my friend was explaining the wisdom of her coworker, she told of how this person would write lists fairly regularly. She would list positive attributes of others and write "why I like you" lists to others. She gave these lists to her colleagues and friends, and they often kept them in their possession, as my friend does. How wonderful to be able to take out a little sheet of paper, perhaps when you are feeling down, and be reminded of your strengths.

This led me to recall the Christmas gifts I gave my sisters, brothers-in-law, and mother several years ago. When my husband first started getting ill about three years ago, we were financially strapped with medical bills. Even though we have medical insurance, there was still so much they didn't cover or denied us. As a result, one of my sisters thought we should not exchange Christmas gifts with one another that year. Still, I wanted to give my family, who had been giving me so much by helping in various ways, something special. I decided to type up words that spoke of them. Each word I chose was very deliberate. The word had to be descriptive of their personality, or it had to remind me of them for some direct reason. Some of the words were dead giveaways, but others you would have to consider a little longer as to why I chose them. I placed these words on a decorative piece of paper and laminated them. After wrapping them up and sending them along, I hoped, just as my friend's friend probably did, that these words would remind my family of their strengths. I'm not sure what impact my gift had on them. Did they return to their lists when feeling down, or did the list bring a smile to their faces on occasion? I do know, though, that I was able to tell them in my own way what I thought of them and how they are important to me. That was a gift to me in and of itself.

LESSON #4

The American Medical System Really Has Problems

❖

What an eye-opening experience these past years have been, going through them from an "ill" perspective rather than a "healthy with check-ups" or "pregnant and having a baby" stance. Prior to Jim's illness, I had only seen hospitals as a few days stopover for having a baby or for visiting a temporarily sick family member. Nothing serious. I had only been to doctors' offices with babies and toddlers for immunizations and wellness visits. I had only been myself for a flu shot or a pap smear and Ob-Gyn visits. Nothing serious.

But then the world turned on a dime, and physicians started acting strange, paperwork mounted, health insurance companies refused to pay for medication and procedures, and forms would show up for payment with a physician's name I had never seen and multiple codes and dates I couldn't keep track of. I began to understand how insurance fraud could happen easily. How could anyone keep up with all this? Why did it have to be so complicated?

My first shattered illusion of the medical world came when Jim and I faced physician after physician who simply wanted to pass Jim off. His symptoms were too strange. He didn't fit into a neat box. I was naïve enough several years ago to think that some physician would be excited by the mystery of Jim's case. That a researcher would take on his cause and be thrilled for the challenge that Jim's case offered. Then the reality set in. Most physicians couldn't spend much time with Jim. They had other patients to see. His case was too involved and couldn't be handled in a thirty-minute visit. There were the physicians who thought Jim was too young (at the time, he was in his late forties) for such problems. Many of these same physicians insisted that Jim was fine, making too much of "getting older" pains. On the other extreme, we had the physicians who were all doom and gloom. After talking with Jim for fifteen minutes, taking a few minor measurements of heart rate, knee reflex responses, and breathing tests, they declared that Jim most likely had ALS, or Lou Gehrig's disease, and therefore two to five more years to live. This announcement was told so haphazardly and without compassion that most friends, upon learning of the story, could not believe it to be true. Fortunately, Jim and I continued our pursuit, knowing that the ALS diagnosis didn't address all of Jim's symptoms. Although Jim was tired of having to explain and justify his feelings about his illness yet another time, we did finally connect with a physician who was good, genuine, compassionate, and ready for a challenge. He fit the stereotype we have of physicians when we are adolescents: they are all-knowing, ready to help at all costs, and will always be on your side to help you get well.

Over the next several years, we continued to slowly find these now rare gems of physicians. We ultimately had a team of four physicians who were excellent; however, it is sad that it took us years to find them and that there are so few physicians like this left. I do recognize that this statement is not entirely fair, it is more a reflection and comment on the medical system rather than the physicians themselves. There were those physicians who I could sense wanted to know more, ask more questions, and try to help, but their schedules were full, and they had to move on to the next patient. There were those emergency room physicians who awed me with their compassion and ready skills. There were those ICU physicians who had really big hearts and tried as best they could to help Jim in whatever way possible. There was even the physician who made a few house calls when he probably should have been going home to his family and who didn't charge us for the visit because the health insurance company wouldn't cover it. He was simply acting out of kindness.

The system we have in this country is not set up to reward thorough, comprehensive care. It is also not set up to promote wellness and preventative care. It deals, in general, with treating symptoms after the fact in as fast and timely a manner as possible. One illustration of this that still baffles me surrounded Jim's physical and occupational therapy. As Jim's muscles began to atrophy, his ability to do the things he had always done was compromised. Eventually, it became so difficult to move that going somewhere for the therapy was not realistic. This is when we switched to in-home physical therapy, which falls into a different category as far as insurance is concerned. The bottom line is that when one is home-bound, physical therapy can continue only if gains are being made. If a person is maintaining function, mobility, etc. because of physical therapy, it doesn't count. The logic is that at this point, the caregivers can assist with the patient's exercises and, therefore, the physical therapists are not necessary. The problem with this, however, is twofold. First, no matter how much training the caregivers have from these physical therapists before they release the patient, the caregivers are not physical therapists. It is obvious but not to be overlooked. Physical therapists train for years, achieve advanced degrees, and can modify and tweak exercises as they see subtle differences in their patients; in short they have experience and traits that caregivers do not typically have. Secondly, the logic that progress in strength or mobility has to be achieved to retain physical therapy is faulty. When the physical therapy stopped, even with the nurses and me helping Jim with his exercises, Jim started to slide backwards. With the physical therapy, Jim maintained muscles and mobility. Without the therapy, he declined. It is precisely the type of evidence that justifies physical therapy in the first place, but again, insurance ignores this and will not cover the visits and costs.

Another area of the medical field that became highlighted to me over the years is the craziness of how reporting, filing, and reimbursements are made. I would receive EOBs (estimates of benefits) from our insurance company. The dates of services on the forms were sometimes from months prior. The physicians' names (which may have been associated with the hospital visits, even though it was no physician we actually saw) were sometimes unrecognizable. The same visit or service would be repeated multiple times on multiple months of EOB statements. There was no way to adequately keep up with this unless I organized things myself in spreadsheet form. And, frankly, there were a lot of visits, services, and tests to keep track of. With two small children to tend to, a husband to care for, and a full-time job to engage in, this was low on my priority list. Still, it was obviously important for me to do so, and I did the best I could, but it was mostly a "by faith" process. I trusted the statements and paid when they told me I owed money.

And, of course, there was the money itself. There were supplies we received from the home-health agency that were so outrageously priced it was hard to believe. In most instances, we were fortunate enough in this area that our insurance company paid in full for these supplies; however, there was the occasional time when something was miscoded or misfiled, and after months of calling people, filling out forms, calling other people, and writing letters, the mistake was finally corrected. Even when things went smoothly, there were things I thought didn't make sense economically. I'm not arguing about the costs of a physician's visit, hospital procedures, and the like. I don't know enough about such matters to have an opinion. I know specialized pieces of equipment are expensive, and costs need to be appropriately applied. I am talking about the medicine given at the hospital that cost $250 when, if I brought in Jim's medicine from home, would be only ten dollars. I'm talking about the sterile swabs to clean around Jim's trach opening in his throat that are basically big, long Q-tips that have been individually sealed in packets to keep them sterile, costing $200 for a box of fifty. These prices would make me cringe, as I knew they contributed to what I had been hearing on the news about the inflation of medical care and coverage.

Blog Entry, April 26, 2013:
Has the Medical Community Gone Totally Insane?

It is truly remarkable how many hours, weeks, and months I spent trying to sort through items related to my husband's medical condition. Because my husband Jim cannot talk or use his hands easily, I am the person who needs to answer questions, fill out forms, call (endlessly) for help, etcetera. Every time there is a new bill or form that comes in the mail, my heart sinks. Not only is it depressing, it is also daunting, energy draining, and frustrating (to say the least). My latest months-long adventure has been so unbelievable that I needed to share it with you.

To make a very long story short, when Jim went on long-term disability we were forced to go on Medicare. We still have our private insurance, which now is considered secondary, and we still pay the same amount of money for the policy (it hasn't gone down even though we now have Medicare as our primary). Well, the complications, pains, and frustrations that come with this change of status are mind-blowing. Everything takes forever, and the rules about what "you didn't have to pay for before" and "sorry, you now have to pay for" make no sense (and they are always changing).

A year ago Jim was rushed to the emergency room—a scary time that fortunately turned out to be only a scare. While Jim was there, he had a chest x-ray, received medication for anxiety, got rehydrated, and took Combivent—basically the inhalers that many people take who have breathing problems such as asthma. Things went back and forth among the hospital, Medicare, the private insurance company, and us. I never knew what was happening. I had to make countless phone calls and wait on things to be mailed to me. Medicare couldn't send paperwork directly to the hospital or the insurance company because apparently they had done it already, and the rule says "only to the patient" after that. So more weeks went by, more months . . .

A year later (yes, a year) I think I finally have things figured out. I receive my new letters from Medicare and can proceed with some knowledge, so I call the hospital. Speaking to a very kind woman, she tells me the balance on our account is now zero. I am so relieved. I still don't really understand what had happened, but I decide not to press my luck and just go with it. Then she tells me the problem was over Medicare's new rules about self-administered drugs. Anything that is placed in your eyes, nose, mouth, or ears is considered self-administered, and Medicare won't pay for it.

My obvious next question was, "What did Jim get that was self-administered?" She told me she couldn't tell me on the phone, but that she could mail me the summary sheet of all the expenses Jim tallied up on that visit. The itemized summary came days later (something I had never seen in the year of trying to sort this out—a point interesting in and of itself). The price of the self-administered drug was $1,559. When I looked to see what it was, it read, "ipratropium albuterol sulfate." I googled this and was absolutely, totally, and completely stunned. It is Combivent ("puffers" or "inhalers" as many people call it). I have a copay of sixty dollars on this when I pick it up at the pharmacy. The hospital was charging close to sixteen hundred dollars for the two or three puffs they gave Jim when he was in the hospital.

I do believe the healthcare industry has gone completely mad. How can this be justified or explained? It is not logical. It is definitely crazy.

Lesson #5

Live Life in the Present

I think of all the lessons I learned or was reminded of over these past many years, this particular one is the most difficult to adapt overall. I know that it is true and yet it is easy to slip down the "what if I did this earlier" mentality, beating yourself up for the regrets or the mistakes you may have made. And it is just as easy to riddle oneself with anxiety over the future unknowns. Still, the only thing we have for absolute sure is the present day, and God's grace is enough for us one day at a time.

During my adolescence, we were required to learn the Lord's Prayer from an early age. We recited the prayer during church and throughout the year at various times. It became second-nature and repeated without the true reflection on the words themselves that should have been in place. Today, I think much more about this prayer and the specific words Jesus chose. For me, there are three striking parts to the prayer:

- The beginning states "Our Father" or as Jesus would have spoken, "Abba," an intimate Hebrew word expressing Dad or Daddy. When Jesus spoke these words he intended for us to know that God was our heavenly daddy; He was accessible to us, and loving; not the formal standoff disciplinarian that had been implied and certainly what I associate with the term "father."

- The prayer also states "give us our daily bread" to remind us that God will give us what we need on a *daily* basis (not weekly or annually). Every day is a new opportunity for God to help us and provide for us, and we must trust that; we must know that. We need to accept that God will give us the grace to make it one day at a time. He will give us what we need, not necessarily what we want, and He will give us the ability to handle some very difficult situations one day at a time.
- The toughest part of the prayer is when we say "Thy will be done on Earth as it is in Heaven." The idea here is obviously for us to give things over to the Lord. Give Him our problems, our concerns, our hopes, frustrations, struggles, cares, and desires. Give it up to Him fully and let it go so that *His* will is done, not our will. There is so much power in this if we are able to do this. But of course, we like to be in control of our own lives, and trusting someone we can't see and having faith in the process is extremely difficult.

Still, when you couple all the parts of the Lord's Prayer together and when you try to live in the moment without the context of yesterday's mistakes or what you should or should not have done and without the context of worrying about tomorrow, you gain freedom. You gain perspective. You gain power.

Reflections throughout the day, on the order of five to ten minutes can serve the purpose of calling you into the present. You can train yourself to be even more disciplined with this process of focusing on the present through meditation. Formal meditation practice has always been very intriguing to me, and the mental and physical benefits of such practices have been documented. Recently, I have begun such a formal practice with the Raleigh Meditation Center. With guided help in the room,

I have been able to pull up memories that have been buried deep within and release them. I have learned to focus on the present so that the memories of the past have no relevance today. These memories only get "fed" if I give them that power. I have been taught through meditation to care not about potential scary future events because they have obviously not occurred, but instead I can concentrate only on the present day and do the best I can with that day. I have been reminded through the meditation process that there is good to see in everything and everyone and that we are all connected. If you can release the negative values and thoughts associated with memories or anxieties over future events, your mind is free and you can connect with a higher power, God. You have power in the present with this, an open mind, and freedom to live in a joyful state.

Blog Entry, September 19, 2012:
Get Over It Already

I know everyone has them. Bad days can sometimes turn into bad weeks. I know it happens to everyone. Still doesn't make me feel better. Well, maybe a little. But not much.

I am just tired. So very tired.

My bad week started with one of our long-time nurses, who we depend on very much, not showing up one morning. He was "over" (as he put it) the nursing company, and had quit. But we suffered, scrambling around to find coverage, me serving as the nurse once again. Not that I mind, of course. I love taking care of my husband. But it's a lot when you throw in the other stuff. Like picking up a sick child and trying to tend to his needs. Needing to pick up milk, butter, and medicine for your husband but not being able to leave the house. Then there are the constant phone calls. "Who is going to pick up this shift?" "What are we going to do about X?" "Let me try to get through to the insurance company." There are always calls, never a break. And then the bills—new ones this week for a new round of IV antibiotics that is not covered by insurance. More supplements, more over-the-counter medicine. Hundreds and hundreds of dollars later, I wonder how I'm going to pay for the electric bill.

Then, on top of all that, just when I think the tide is turning, something else happens. My husband had a doctor's appointment this morning. The new nurse helped get Jim ready and down the stairs. I had phoned a handicapped van service to pick us up. I dropped off my daughter at a neighbor's house (my sick son is still with me today), and I'm thinking all is going well and things are taken care of. Jim was going to get something done at the doctor's office that should help him. Okay, it is going to be a good day. Minutes after the van should be here, it is not. I call. The driver is on his way. More minutes go by. Finally, it is here and Jim is being loaded into the van. My cell phone rings and I look at the number—my heart sinks. It's the doctor's office. "Erica, where are you?" the nurse asks. "We are four minutes out—max. The van just got here to pick us up." I plead with her to let us come. A kind person, she puts me on hold to see if the doctor can still squeeze Jim in. He can't. I guess the good news is that I didn't have to pay for the trip. So, we unload Jim and frustration abounds.

I'm trying to get over it. I am. But the only time Jim can be squeezed in before the doctor is off for training and conferences is Saturday morning. Of course we take the appointment. Sadly, it's the same time as my son's soccer game. I had to miss the game last week. He had to miss practice on Monday (because I was the nurse that day.) I am just so tired of shuffling things and asking friends for favors. But I do ask, because frankly I have no other choice. I am blessed that my friends are so generous with their time.

So I'm trying to get over it. I decided a Venti skim chai latte from Starbucks will help. It does a little. As I drive back from Starbucks, I try all the other things I know that have helped me in the past: I try to focus on something to be grateful for today; I try to recite some scripture; I try to shift my mood by listening to an inspiring song. Nothing is working. I am frustrated and tired of everything being dictated to me.

I return home and see my sick son resting on the chair, watching television, and my husband is sitting next to him in his wheelchair. Not an ideal situation for either one of them. My son doesn't feel well, and Jim is not in his bedroom, where he feels most comfortable, he is in the wheelchair that causes him pain and unable to efficiently call for help when he needs it.. Still, what a heartwarming sight. The two most important men in my life, hanging out, bonding in a way that so many of us take for granted. I smile and am happy for the moment.

Maybe the tides are turning.

LESSON #6

WHEN GOD ANSWERS PRAYERS, HE SENDS PEOPLE

All my life my mother told me that if I were good and kind to people, positive things would happen in my life. This is related to the whole karma business: what goes around, comes around, so to speak. While I'm not sure of this, there is wisdom in the saying. We should all certainly try to be kind to one another and hope that the good guys win in the end.

Still, there are good people that get the short end of the stick. There are bad things that happen to good people. There is unfairness when we desire justice.

I have come to learn that although I cannot explain or understand the bad things and why these bad things may happen, there is power in praying and waiting. The timing of events, circumstances, and answers will not necessarily be what or when we want—at least very rarely. But knowing that we can persevere and wait patiently helps put adversity in perspective. Knowing that God is on our side and working all things for good is a lifesaving rope when we are drowning. The blessing of people that comes when prayers are answered should be a reminder that we are not alone, and although no bad event can ever be fully understood, something good can be found even in the most challenging times.

There was one series of events that transpired over the last year of Jim's life. It was no accident, and it was the culmination of many prayers: physical help for Jim, reminders to Jim of his worth, mental stimulation for Jim, and inspiration for perseverance.

The series of events started with Jim's in-home physical therapy being dropped due to Jim's status: he wasn't making adequate gains in strength and therefore insurance wouldn't cover the visits. The nurses and I did our best to help with the exercises, but frankly, he could too readily disregard a nurse or me. "I'm tired, Erica," Jim would say, "Let's do it in another hour." By then the kids needed attention, dinner had to be made, and other such matters distracted me from helping Jim with his exercises. When I finally returned, Jim had cycled back to being exhausted, and the day was nearly over.

When family suggested asking friends and neighbors to act as the therapists and provide outsider motivation, I decided to ask for help. The first time I did this there weren't any takers. Several months went by until another hospital visit with therapy ended too soon. I put out another call for interest. This is when Brian, a friend from church, responded that he and some of the guys he exercised with were happy to help. These men belonged to a group called F3—signifying fitness, faith, and fellowship. Brian spearheaded the cause, coming at the tail end of the physical therapists' sessions to get trained. Then Brian trained the other men in the group. They set up rotations of men to visit with Jim and help him with his exercises. They treated Jim as one of their group, not as a sick man like many people were inclined to do. They told jokes, prayed with Jim, and urged him on. They stepped in at a time when Jim's mental health was shaky and he was feeling abandoned by friends. They stepped in to remind him that he was loved, he was capable, and he mattered.

Toward the end of Jim's life, when he was no longer able to exercise, the F3 men continued to visit. They had music jam sessions to cheer Jim's spirits. They told stories. They came one afternoon en masse and filled every corner of Jim's room to pray and be with him.

During these last several months of Jim's life, these men made all the difference in the world to Jim and my family. They were the answers to our prayers for help. They were the reminder that we were not alone and that God was present in a variety of ways.

July 2014: A Portion of Brian's Eulogy at Jim's Funeral

My name is Brian, but I'm also known as Tony Robbins to the men of F3. F3 stands for fitness, fellowship, and faith. We are a free, participant-led workout group with a mission to plant, grow, and serve small workout groups for the invigoration of male community leadership. Every participant gets an F3 name or handle—a nickname, if you will.

Jim Young was as much a part of F3 as any of us, and his F3 name came from one of his favorite movies, Shawshank Redemption, and its title character, Andy Dufresne, played by Tim Robbins. If you've seen the movie, there is a scene near the end where Red, played by Morgan Freeman, has left prison and is reading a letter Andy left for him. In the letter, Andy states, "Hope is a good thing, maybe the best of things, and no good thing ever dies." So Jim's F3 name is Dufresne, and that line from the movie became our mantra for working out with Jim. In part, that clip helped inspire what we called the workouts—Hopebuilder. Hopebuilder grew over time with more men coming to work out with Jim. We were all out of our comfort zones, and Dufresne handled our ineptitude with good humor. Knowing Jim, that's not surprising, but if you saw us coming, you'd really be in for a laugh. A group of Type A personalities, not known for their exceptional communication skills or willingness to ask for help, leading workouts focused on physical therapy. Again, not a single one of us had PT training, but that didn't stop us or dampen our enthusiasm. To illustrate our enthusiasm and Jim's good humor, Jim was in an easy lift recliner, which we adjusted from time to time to position him for different exercises. On this particular day, four F3 men, all attorneys, joined Dufresne for a workout. One attorney managed to unknowingly turn on the vibrate function of the chair. For a good while, only Dufresne knew this and was trying every way he knew how to let the guys know he wanted them to turn it off. Picture four attorneys standing around a chair, trying to figure

out how to turn this thing off, talking over one another, and trying to communicate with Dufresne throughout the whole
ordeal. So the question remains: how many attorneys does it
take to turn off the vibrate function of an easy lift chair? The
world may never know. They had to call in the nurse for help,
a sad moment of defeat for the men of F3. Jim was patient
throughout and shot us one of his smiles afterwards. You all
know the one.

The objective of Hopebuilder changed with the circumstances, from seeing Dufresne stand on his own in February to
simply providing camaraderie and support to Jim's family when
he became terminally ill.

As Will (F3 name, Maize) eloquently shared with F3 earlier this week, "Jim left a great impression on those who visited
him and worked out with him. None of us knew Jim before he
contracted chronic Lyme disease, and his situation was difficult
to comprehend. Even without the benefit of the past you could
just tell that Jim was a great person who positively impacted
many wherever he went. What he was dealt struck me as cruel
and unfair. I should be more at peace with it now, but candidly
I'm not. He would have loved F3 in the gloom, as we know it.
Jim sure loved it in the form we provided. When we were in his
room assisting with the exercises, the presence of God was evident and powerful, and these were some of the most significant
moments I can ever recall. Those memories have helped. That
and the clear recognition that what Jim went through was not
in vain."

We are all better for having had the opportunity to get to
know Jim Young. Jim's legacy in F3 Raleigh will be as significant as anyone, because his needs rallied the core participants
unlike anything else, and the timing of local growth accelerating
with these workouts was not a coincidence. What's a better
example of servant leadership than men collaborating (with no
professional experience) to help someone get better?
Hopebuilder was F3 in its purest form striking hard on all 3 Fs.

So a few things we men of F3 have learned and are grateful to Jim, Erica, and their family for:

From David (F3 name, Fazio): That friendship and brotherhood are deepened when we share each other's burdens as we were called to do. Most of all, Jim's fight was tangible proof of the promise of Romans 5:2b–5: "And we boast in the hope of the glory of God. Not only so, but we also glory in our sufferings, because we know that suffering produces perseverance; perseverance, character; and character, hope. And hope does not disappoint us, because God's love has been poured out into our hearts through the Holy Spirit, who has been given to us."

From Mike (F3 name, Minnie): Erica has shown the importance of communication and the written word. Through her blog, she has opened her home and life to so many. She could have very easily closed down and walled off her family to society while they dealt with the pain. She chose the exact opposite and opened up, humbled her family, and asked for help from God and others. Knowing we all have limitations, we can take from this that we all need help from time to time and it's incumbent upon us as humans and Christians to seek those in need to offer a helping hand and our Father's grace.

From John (F3 name, Cinderella): Dufresne taught me that that the fewer words you speak, the more those words mean.

From Lee (F3 Name, Slash): I will always remember Jim's hearty welcome to F3. Even in his final days he wanted to be part of the F3 brotherhood—bad jokes, bad nicknames, bad backs, bad singing, and warm hearts.

From Mark (F3 name, Steroid): I learned that in the face of seemingly insurmountable obstacles, it is possible to push yourself, be positive, and to set goals. I was inspired by Jim's spirit, and it taught me that faith can move mountains and provide hope where usually there is none.

Simply put, Jim Young brought all of us who came in contact with him and his family, whether through workouts, visits, or through Erica's blog posts, closer to God. He taught us that we need God and one another. We all need community. We are not meant to go through this life on our own. Jim helped us, many of whom he never met, grow closer to God and one another. In a real and meaningful way, Jim helped us focus on the right priorities, and for many of us, changed our perspective, for which we are most grateful. In the words of Henry David Thoreau, "It's not what you are looking at that matters, it's what you see."

As Wes, (F3 name White Shoe), shared early on, "It's going to be a great day when Jim joins us on the field for an F3 workout." Those of us in F3 have discussed how great a day it will be when we arrive in heaven to work out with Jim in the body his heavenly Father has prepared for him.

Words of Insight from My Children

Braxton and Annalise have experienced many things during their formative years, which most of their peers have not experienced. They have experienced loss and sadness over a father who could not engage with them as any of us would like. They have faced uncertainty surrounding their future. They have handled many parent figures present at different times throughout the year, probably giving them different messages that could be confusing. But they have also experienced many wonderful things. They have seen kindness and love in action in so many ways over the years.

My son, who is now nine years old, experienced a healthy Dad for the first one and half years of his life, a struggling father for the next several, and then a declining and very ill father for the rest of their time together. My son was seven years old when Jim died (just shy of turning eight). My daughter, who is now six years old, has never known a healthy father. She was born when Jim's treatments for neurological chronic Lyme disease started in full force. She had some moments with him, but much of their interaction occurred with house guests, nurses, and machinery forming a blockade around them.

Still, my kids have learned many valuable life lessons. They have seen love given to both their daddy, their family in general, and unbelievable acts of kindness to remind them that there is always good present, even in the middle of tragedy and hard times. They have engaged with strangers at first, friends later, who have come with open hearts to help. They have learned much about perseverance from watching their daddy, and they have embraced God and Jesus in a way that I don't think they would have without Jim's illness and death defining their early lives.

When I asked the kids if they wanted to help with the book, I was pleasantly taken back by their enthusiasm. They were eager to give back some guidance to others and offer what in some instances blew me away as very sophisticated thoughts. Below are the words they want to share.

- "Don't waste your life on Earth and do all the good stuff in Heaven. Savor your life on Earth and stay holy." –Braxton, age eight.
- "Spend more time with your family because you never know how much time you will get with them." –Braxton.
- "Just because something happens to you doesn't mean it should haunt you for the rest of your life." –Braxton.
- "Just because someone can't do things, it doesn't mean they are a different type of person." –Braxton.
- "Just because your mom or dad dies doesn't mean you're going to have a new one. You will always have your real mom or dad in your heart." –Braxton.
- "When someone dies, it doesn't mean you can walk and say 'I don't love you.' It means you don't have to be scared of them." –Annalise, age six.

Upon reflecting on my children's comments, it became evident that my list of what they have learned also needs to include the value of each and every person. Every person matters. Every person's life has meaning. There is power in realizing that a person matters. Through empathy and kindness, my children have learned that it is possible to always be a victor rather than becoming a victim. I so appreciate that my kids want to share this lesson with others. If you reread their list with this idea in mind, you will see the list in a new light.

When Braxton was about five years old, he spoke to me about a song he was writing. He insisted on working on his piece for days at a time. He dictated what to write since he was not able to write his thoughts down quickly enough (and in a matter that he would later be able to decipher). He asked me to reread his words and then tweak and change them until his song was perfect. He spent so long on the song that it was no longer necessary to reread the words —they had been memorized. Next, he sang the song and did a dance to go along with it. His song is telling.

"Believe in Yourself" by Braxton Young (age five)
You can do anything for me or you.
It's okay if you win or lose.
It's okay if you matter fact or lose.
It's okay if you don't win or lose.
You just need to believe in yourself.
Just believe in yourself
For me and you.
Just believe in yourself.
So don't fail.
It's okay if you don't do everything you want to.
Just believe in yourself.
It's a matter of fact to lose.
Just don't worry about anything.
Just believe in yourself.
It's okay if you don't break a record.
Just believe in yourself.

Several years later, when Braxton was eight, he updated this song. It's interesting that the theme is consistent.

"Believe," by Braxton Young (age eight)
I just want to say
That if you think you can do something
Then you should try to do it.
Do not think about anything that people say,
Just believe in yourself and try again,
And again.
Some people say you can't do things,
Just put that behind you
And do what you think you can do.
For example, if someone says
You can't spell something
That doesn't mean you can't,
So just give it a shot.
Now that you have done it,
You should try something else.
You just have to believe in yourself.
Like I do.
You can do anything if you believe in yourself.
Anyone can do that.
Like you can climb Mount Everest if you believe.
Just believe.
Just believe.

Braxton also wrote another song entitled "Hiding in your Heart," age eight

Oh, oh, oh, oh, oh
You have to try to get your way.
You have to try.
But if you don't succeed you have to try again and again.
But you have to try for the sake of God and for us.
You have to succeed.
But in the secret of your heart you have to be fighting.
I know you are.
You have to tell me.
For the sake of God,
You have to try.
I know you're hiding something in your heart.
You have to try.

One evening, not long after he wrote this song, Braxton was in deep thought mode. "What is on your mind, little boy?" I asked. "I'm thinking about Daddy," he replied. When I asked him to say more, he got out a pen and paper and crafted the following poem.

You are my flashlight
You get me through the dark and into the light
Every night I know you are there
Because you are the light of me.
You get me through the night to the light
And now I stand here looking at you
Because you got me through the night
Because you are my flashlight
And now I want to say one thing:
You are the light of me
And every step I look for you
Because you got me from the dark to the light
Because you are the light of me,
Of me.

LESSON #7

GRATITUDE IS ONE OF THE KEYS TO JOY

I learned years ago that happiness and joyfulness are two separate things.

Happiness is dictated by happenings and is, therefore, temporary in nature. Happiness will come and go just as events come and go. In my opinion, happiness is externally driven and relies too much on things other than ourselves.

Joyfulness is just the opposite. Joy is internal and something that can be called from within as the need arrives. Joy comes from the power of remembering, recalling, and focusing on that which is good. This is where gratitude comes into play.

It is not a coincidence that almost any article we read, presentation we hear, or book we read dedicated to the subject of resilience, life after tragedy, or overcoming obstacles mentions the power of gratitude. Gratitude allows us to shift our focus to that which really matters. To shift our energy to a place of refueling rather than draining. To gain perspective when everything around us seems a blur. To find peace in the chaos.

Sometimes finding something good to focus our thoughts on can be difficult, especially when life is seemingly terribly unfair. Even if it is just a nugget of good, you can find something of value. Something positive. As we work to focus every day on finding that which to be grateful for, we learn that there is much. It is constant. It is always present.

I also learned that outwardly expressing gratitude shifts things even more. By verbalizing gratitude in some way, another dimension of joy is added. We can say words out loud to acknowledge gratitude. This is something I have done repetitively over the years with the kids to try and highlight the good that is present in our lives. We could write what we are most grateful for privately in a journal. Others like to blog or write more public articles on the topic. Regardless of the format, there is something about being active with our gratitude that helps our minds find the joy that is present in our lives.

People learn more and understand more if they are engaged in several ways with the material. That is, if there are different modalities involved, people will internalize material more effectively. This is what neuroscientists have found. This is what educational researchers have documented. Working in multiple formats to acknowledge and express gratitude in a variety of ways is no different. The more approaches we take, the easier it will be for us to draw on that joy and focus on what is truly important in life. Gratitude provides perspective. Gratitude can save our lives.

**Blog Entry, August 31, 2012: Genuine Friends
and the Benefit of Hanging Out**

A vacation of any sort is good for the soul. The recent trip I took with my two small children to Michigan to visit my family was a good break. My kids had a fantastic time with their cousins, and I was able to hang out and do normal things, something I miss on a regular basis. Because my husband is so ill, my days are usually filled with tending to his needs and the needs of our family, so there is usually very little time left for hanging out. While in Michigan, I tried to savor these experiences. One afternoon, we all went to Lake Michigan. I watched with such joy as my kids buried each other in the sand, threw balls on the beach, and froze their toes off going into the cold water. That night, we had a campfire, drank wine, and talked about all kinds of things. Another afternoon we watched a niece participate in an Irish dance competition and then visited my alma mater, Michigan State University. We walked by the river, had lunch in a restaurant, and drove around campus. Other days we visited the zoo, fished, and went tubing in the lake; in general, we just hung out. It felt good to be in this relaxed environment, woes temporarily on the back burner.

One evening, a high school buddy came over for a visit. It had been several years since we'd seen one another. The last time was at a high school reunion where talking one-on-one is often minimal because people are so excited to see as many old friends as possible. It was great to talk with my friend during this past trip, just hanging out in my sister's backyard, drinking a beer, and laughing. It was as if we spoke on a regular basis, without much time passing since the last time. I was reminded of my friend's genuineness, her infectious smile, and her overall kindness. It occurred to me, upon reflection of the night, that I am most fortunate in many ways. Here was this person, after so many years, still so lovely. I know that if I need her, I can call. I know she would be willing to help. I know that she cares about my family and me. What a gift that is.

It also occurred to me as I was reflecting upon the trip and my experiences in general that I really do have many kind friends and family helping at almost every turn. If I ask, someone is there for my family. I hope that other people facing such adversity have these connections in their lives. I can't imagine how I would be able to cope with my husband's life-threatening illness if I didn't have this support.

Once my kids and I returned from our short trip, a friend saved me again. Based on a new antibiotic regime, my husband is being hit hard and is incredibly weak. He cannot stand on his own, walk, or breathe without assistance. He is struggling a great deal mentally as well. One night he began talking about his death. It was almost unbearable to consider life without Jim, and I too struggled mentally. After a long sleepless night filled with many tears, Jim's life-long friend from Alabama called on the phone. We had a conversation that helped me greatly, and his words were enough of a pick-me-up that I could continue to help Jim and try to get him back on track.

Upon writing this, I realize that Jim and I both certainly know how to pick friends. Our world is most definitely a better place because of them.

LESSON #8

THERE IS EVIL IN THE WORLD AND NOT EVERYTHING HAPPENS FOR A REASON

❖

When I was in college, one of my best friends and I were simultaneously (and coincidentally) breaking up with our boyfriends. To help us through the pain we would chant, "Everything happens for a reason, and if it was meant to be, it will be, and that's what we have to figure out." I moved through my early years of adulthood with that same attitude. There was a reason why my friend moved out of state, why I went to a particular graduate school, why I lost touch with that particular friend, etc.

I learned, however, that this was far too simplistic a view. While it is true that there are instances when premonitions or people come our way at the times we need a message, it's not true that all of the workings of the universe are happening for the good. There is evil in the world and sometimes very bad things happen to good people. There are many unfair, horrible things that happen to good people. There is no sugar coating a rape, a tsunami, a long-term illness, a premature death—you get the picture.

When people casually said things like, "Look on the bright

47

side" or "Everything happens for a reason," it would sting something fierce.

I think it was extra painful because ever since I can remember, starting in my teenage years, I held this same view, this preconceived mantra. But how can we explain away some of the things I mentioned? How can I say that my children's father died for a reason? They are growing up without his love, his guidance, his support, and his wisdom. There is no reason for this. Period.

We can take a tragic event, however, and choose to focus on something of value that comes from it. My kids have been shown love and kindness from all walks of life. My kids have had persistence and grace modeled to them by their father. I have learned some valuable lessons that I know have made me a better person, and I hope I can pass them along to my children. I try to remember, some days are easier than others, that God can use even the worst events for ultimate good. Consider Romans 8:28: "And we know that in all things God works for the good of those who love him, who have been called according to his purpose."

I also learned over the years that there is an evil force at work in our world and there are bad people and bad spirits who aim to destroy. If we don't have that realism behind us, we will struggle to understand, and we will get stuck in the victim category. Thoughts like, "Why me?" and "Everything bad always seems to happen to me" are easy to adopt if we can't recognize our own ability to pull out of a bad situation and realize that sometimes bad is coming because it is bad. If we ignore that there is evil in the world, we cannot recognize it or fight it by keeping our mind focused where it should be or keep control of our lives.

As I moved through Jim's illness and death, I was drawn to the story of Joseph from the Old Testament. We all remember the man whose father showed such favoritism that he made a special coat of rainbow colors for his son. His brothers hated him as a result of this (among other things, like Joseph's dreams, which he shared with his brothers) and eventually the brothers sold him into slavery. In Egypt, Joseph persisted, focused on the good present, but again was betrayed, thrown in prison, and forgotten. He was released to help decipher the Pharaoh's dreams and did such a fantastic job that Pharaoh made him the top man in the country. Once the great famine started, everyone outside of Egypt was struggling and starving. Eventually, Joseph's brothers made the trip to Egypt in order to see the man in charge, the man who could help them and provide food, the man they did not recognize as their brother. But, why would they? Joseph now looked, acted, and spoke like a powerful Egyptian. Although the brothers did not recognize Joseph, he recognized them. Joseph, rather than seeking revenge, decided to focus on the good and helped the brothers (through a series of manipulations) to realize their evil ways. Joseph could have even forgiven the brothers and given them food and sent them on their way, but he knew if he did this, the brothers would still be in trouble with God and their futures. It would be a different kind of trouble, one with far more severe consequences. After he helped the brothers become mentally healthy and in good relations with God, Joseph did reveal his identity and continued to go out of his way to treat his family and their descendants as royalty. This series of events saved Israel.

During that revelation period, when Joseph finally exposed himself to his brothers, he commented: "You intended to harm me, but God intended it for good to accomplish what is now being done, the saving of many lives." Genesis 50:20

This story has been instrumental in my understanding and remembrance that God can take the bad and eventually make it work for good. While I do not know what this good might be from my current situation of losing my husband and father to my children, I am confident there is good working. This thought puts things in perspective and helps me deal with any sadness or bad day that comes my way.

Blog Entry, June 19, 2014: When Mean Girls Become Mean Women

Do you remember that movie Mean Girls with Lindsay Lohan about how awful high school girls can be to one another? Well, I never really thought much about what happens to such girls as they age; however, I was reminded about this phenomenon the other week and got to experience a mean girl now as a mean woman.

She wore a green dress. She was accessorized by a male who had his arm around her waist the entire night. She was also accessorized by a glare that seemed to say, "Back off, I'm important." My date to a fancy school fundraiser event that evening was one of my friends who decided I needed a night out on the town. My husband is now under Hospice care, and she knew I could use a night to be a "normal" person. It would be good to get out for a few hours, laugh, and have some good food and drink. My night prior to meeting up with the mean woman in green was just that: relaxing and fun.

Several other friends came to the fundraiser event. There were many sweet couples out on dates that night. I was sad that my night was without my husband. It has been like this for years now, but recently it has been different. I feel increasingly sad as his health declines more and more. In the past, my husband would have been with me at such a function. He would have been full of life, but now he lies in a bed unable to communicate, move, or breathe on his own.

And so, as with life in general over these past many years, I smiled through the pain, I concentrated on the positive, and I was grateful for all that I have. I do have so much.

In an ironic twist, the mean woman reminded me again of what I have to be grateful for. After a period of mingling, speeches began. There was talking in the back of the room. I sat between the talkers and the mean woman in green. She glanced back often, throwing daggers with her eyes if you were paying attention. It seemed that I was the only person who noticed her. Our eyes met a few times but I quickly looked away and tried to focus on the speeches. The accessory man pulled the mean woman close, trying to gain her attention. More speakers approached the podium. There was more chatting among the crowd. I could see the mean woman growing more and more agitated as the people in the back of the room laughed louder and louder, and the overall volume in the room increased. I was soaking it all in, my study on human behavior. I was quiet, but then I made a mistake. I looked at my cell phone and laughed at a photo that had been sent to me.   Apparently I laughed too loudly, and I was close enough to the mean woman in green to get a direct hit. I honestly don't remember what she said (other than "Do you mind?"), but I remember her tone, the ugliness of it, and I was struck by the outrageous entitlement she seemed to have given herself to rank above everyone else in the room. I was shocked by her rudeness, to the point I didn't know what to say. My friends, flanking me on my right and left side, stared in amazement too. If I could have looked at their faces, I am sure their eyes would have been bulging just as much as mine. How do women get to act like that? Part of the answer may lie in the fact that she has always acted in such a manner and gotten away with it. The mean girl became the mean woman.

I felt myself shrink as a child would when scolded. But this feeling was soon replaced with gratitude. My friends were outraged for me. They all agreed that the woman's speech was inappropriate and rude. In an expected way, my sadness changed into joy as I was reminded that friends are so important. My next thought centered on the seemingly random attack on me. Of all the people in the room, why did the mean woman in green breathe fire on me when there were plenty of other rule-breakers to the "keep absolutely quiet" rule set by Ms. Queen Bee?

Right at this time, my cell phone buzzed in my purse.

Looking down I noticed it was from my seven-year-old son. I excused myself and walked to the corner of the building. Since it was near the kitchen, there were no party guests hanging about there and it was quiet. After talking to the babysitter, I needed to just be. I was still processing the mean woman's comments. I checked my text messages, answered several of them, checked in on my husband, and fought back the tears. I tried to make sense of it all, but when the chef walked up to me and asked if everything was alright, I knew it was time to return to the scene of the crime.

The mean woman was still there. I considered for a minute if I should say something to her, but decided that was not the point. I didn't know what the point was, so what would I say to her? Ideas like, "Are you really that miserable in life?" or "If you had any idea of what some people were experiencing in life you might think otherwise about acting so hastily and mean" didn't seem like good ideas. Again, I didn't know what my point was, and if someone can't answer that basic question, she has no business taking action. So I just "was" again.

Another friend flagged me over and started bad-mouthing the mean woman in green. She had seen her behavior, too. She also thought it was outrageous. It made me feel good but embarrassed at the same time. Again, why did the mean woman in green pick me? As with much in life these days, I don't know. There are so many things I wish I knew, wish I understood, even a little. There are so many events, people, and comments, that don't make sense. Things I don't understand. I probably never will, but as long as I focus on the good in life, I can move forward. The mean women of the world in green dresses and their counterparts may make me pause, but if they ultimately help flag something of value, like the importance of friends, then I can take the verbal assaults any day.

LESSON #9

JESUS IS NOT ONLY THE SAVIOR OF THE WORLD, HE IS ALSO THE MODEL FOR US ALL

❖❖❖

Jesus was sent from Heaven to be born as an infant, live as a perfect human being, and then die on a cross for the sins of the world. His resurrection sealed our fate that life can be eternal. I have banked on this for as long as I can remember. I find reassurance and contentment knowing Jim is in the intermediate Heaven, thanks to Jesus. Jim is free and capable of doing all sorts of physical things now, such as walking, skiing, and golfing—things he hadn't been able to do over the last few years of his life.

What has been strengthened in me as a result of my journey is certainly my faith, but also the realization that Jesus' life while on Earth should not be glossed over as steps leading to the death and resurrection. Jesus lived for thirty-three or thirty-four years on this planet, and he taught many things over those years. I can recall many parables learned from my childhood of Jesus' teachings—many valuable lessons that we can take to heart. All of these are important. There was nothing Jesus said that wasn't important. Every word spoken from his lips had value.

What I have come to appreciate is that Jesus' life overall is to serve as a model for us. We should aim to consider how Jesus would approach a situation (remember the "What Would Jesus Do" campaign? There was real value with this reflection). We should aspire to use the same tone and kindness toward others, but we should also move to line up our broader perspectives and global thinking to be more like Jesus. I think this is where I have fallen short. I have lived too nearsighted rather than using longer-term vision. I have focused on the practical lessons of Jesus rather than studying the more philosophical teachings. The subtle messages Jesus gave by his words, actions, and in some cases inactions are worth meditation. For example, when Jesus entered a town, he could have cured every sick person in that town if he wanted to; however, he chose not to do so. In one instance in particular, in Nazareth, we are told:

"And because of their unbelief, he couldn't do any miracles among them except to place his hands on a few sick people and heal them." Mark 6:5

I take from this passage many things, but the most obvious to me is that we need to have conviction to the core. We need to passionately believe in things that matter. We need to know that sometimes it's okay not to do everything just because we can. Sometimes there is a good reason to hold back on something. As a mother, this totally resonates with me. There are some occasions where I do not want things to be easy for my kids. They will learn more if they have to figure it out on their own or work harder to accomplish it.

Jesus' life was also about suffering. Not just his time on the cross, of which I cannot fathom the pain. His whole time on Earth was a struggle. He knew hunger, poor living conditions, scorn from people, betrayal from loved ones, mockery, contempt, and even hate directed at him for no good reason. Although he was obviously loved by many people, he was not the embraced figure that so many people today imagine. During his life, Jesus suffered.

This reminder helped me during some of the really hard

months and years of watching Jim suffer. It was almost unbear-able at times to see my husband suffer as he did and feel so help-less in being able to alleviate that suffering. It was hard to see the kids suffering for lack of an intimate connection with their daddy, and I felt the pain of missing my healthy husband and our life together. The reminder that Jesus too suffered helped me through these dark periods. I could remember how Jesus acted and try to model his actions. His acceptance of God's will. His trust in God. His knowledge that there is life after death.

I knew Jesus came to help us and that he is still present today. When Jim was in the last few days of his life here, I cried out to Jesus to help my husband with his suffering. I know he didn't let me down, and that upon his death, Jim instantly was with God and Jesus in heaven.

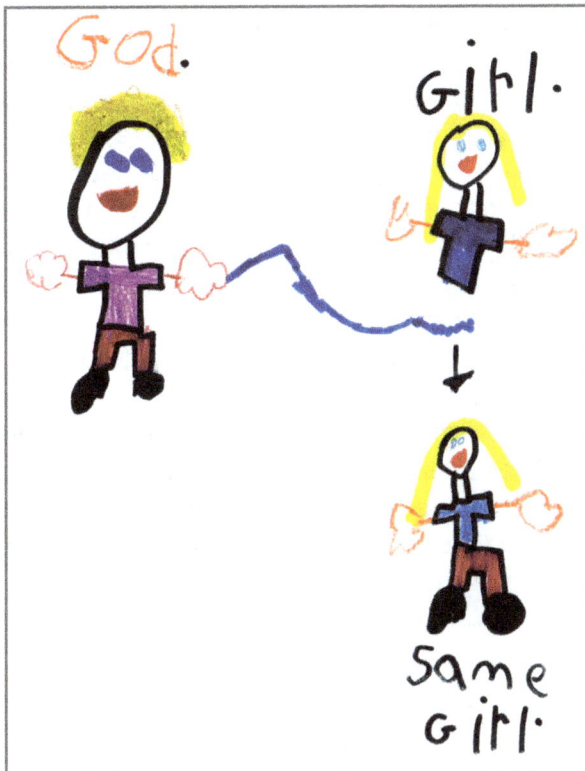

Blog Entry, September 11, 2012: God-Intended Detours

I just finished listening to a sermon by Joel Osteen. One thing he said during the sermon really resonated with me. He made the comment that sometimes detours appear in our journey that seem to lead us away from where we want to be, but that these detours often provide us with valuable insight. If we trust that God is in control and release our desire to micromanage our own lives, then amazing things can start to happen. What might be perceived as a stumbling block could really be a building block leading to success.

The tricky part becomes when to recognize a detour as an opportunity rather than using the detour as a distraction and finding ourselves unable to move on from there. I think Joel Osteen would say, "Let it go, don't worry too much about it. Don't try to overanalyze it. Trust God." I see the value in this— at some point, we need to release things. We may have tried everything we know, and now it may be a matter of trusting things will work out as they should. I also see the value of paying attention to what may be waiting at that detour. For example, is there a stranger who is giving valuable advice? Not acting on the advice may get us stuck at our detour rather than allowing it to serve as the pit stop it was intended to be. This needs to be the time when we follow our gut instincts. These instincts may also be God at work, helping to propel us down the right road, leading us to success.

Rather than hissing at the detours in our journey, greet them as a gift and pay attention to what God has intended us to learn from this temporary stop. This attitude can make our journey during troubled times much more enjoyable as we take and use the gems we are learning along the way.

LESSON #10

WE CANNOT CONTROL ANYTHING

There is freedom coming to this realization and there is power. The desire to help, carve, mold, and control is definitely hard-wired into our human existence. I have never witnessed a person who has been able to freely give up all desire to control his or her life and be at peace with it. We are taught from an early age that we can do anything if we set our minds to it. If we work hard. And there is truth in that statement, up to a point. Nothing will happen because we want it to or because we need it to. Things are ultimately under the control of God. He is with us. He has shown us the way, and He has provided us with amazing insight and guidance when we choose to focus our efforts with Him.

Even though I tried as much as humanly possible, using all the resources I could and asking for all the help that I thought would give Jim the best fighting chance, things were out of my hands. Out of my control. There were several occasions where I was rushing to the hospital, frantic from a phone call I had received from a nurse and not knowing what was happening to Jim. Jim was probably scared, frustrated, and unable to communicate as he would have liked. I had to get to him, and I had to get to him fast. As I pulled into the hospital parking lot and started running to the emergency room, thoughts flashed through my mind: How much more can Jim handle? Why does Jim have to suffer so much? What is physically happening to Jim right now?

During one of these frantic trips, I paused on my way into the building. I stopped. I stopped my crying and my questioning and my racing mind. And then it happened . . . I gave it up and gave it over to God. My comment at that point was, *"Whatever your will is God, I can handle it. The kids and I will be okay. I cannot do anything without You, and this is all for You to decide. Whatever your will."* I didn't like saying these words, but I knew they were true. I could do nothing. I had no control over the situation. I had to trust. Once those words came out, I felt a peace I cannot explain. There was calm. I didn't like giving over the problem to God, but I knew He was the one to take the bad and make the best of it for the best possible outcome, for the most people, over the longest time. I had to trust.

A friend came to visit Jim and me in what turned out to be Jim's last hospital stay in 2014. She said, "Remember, Erica, what is over our heads is under His feet." It was true that I could not understand, but I knew God was present, God was good, and God saw all things in a way that I could not.

". . . the peace of God, which transcends all understanding, will guard your hearts and your minds in Christ Jesus." Philippians 4:7.

I found myself focusing on this scripture verse, reminding me that I couldn't understand, but I could trust; the control I didn't have was present in the form of Jesus and God.

Blog Entry, January 15, 2015: Can a Twenty-Five-Minute Encounter Change One's Life?

The doorbell rang. I was impressed by the punctual arrival. A sweet, elderly lady greeted me with a smile. She had travelled an hour to pick up a hospital bed for her husband. The same one my late husband had used. We went to the garage and I showed her how to put it together (it was in parts for easy mobility), and we talked logistics. Then the question came, "Why are you selling the bed?" I had to explain. I was grateful for the question—so many people avoid talking or asking about Jim these days for fear they will upset me. She looked shocked. I was reminded how shocking it is to learn that neurological Lyme disease can kill a person. Then she told me her story. Her husband had had a stroke. At first the physicians misdiagnosed it as Parkinson's disease. Then, while he was walking in his disabled state, a car struck him. I was horrified for her. We both fought back tears. We talked about the pain of seeing someone you love suffer and the frustration of not being able to help them in the ways we wanted. Then she announced, "Come meet him." I hadn't realized he was in the car. We walked over, and I opened the door. Another lovely, wide, beautiful smile. A face aged by years of doing. Wrinkles, crow's feet, and signs of stress and age on the face. A beautiful face. We chatted for a bit, and then I excused myself so I could get the bed into their van.

After we loaded up the bed, the woman asked, "How much do I owe you?" She pulled out an envelope of cash. "There is no need," I replied. "I hope you enjoy the bed and that it's helpful for your husband." Then I paused and added, "I'm happy it is going to you both. It served Jim well and I hope it does the same for your husband." Again, the woman had the look of shock on her face. "No, I insist I pay you something," she protested. I again said no. Then her tears flowed, and she embraced me with the biggest bear hug I've had in awhile.

"God bless you," she said. "God bless you, too," I replied. She stood back and then came to hug me again, so genuine in her gestures. Several more times she commented "God bless you," and she meant it.

I approached the man again in the passenger seat. His wife told him the bed was a gift. He started tearing up, and then the tears started to fall. The three of us were all there crying with the connection of pain, blessings of having lived good lives, and the frustration that comes with the knowledge that things sometimes go wrong and you can't control them.

As the van drove off and I waved goodbye, tears continued to stream down my face. This couple, elderly and so full of love for each other, had just blessed my life. I was saddened in that I had thought Jim and I would get to that point—be the cute, elderly couple who still enjoyed each other so much. I was glad, though, to have made a small difference in this particular couple's lives.

My twenty-five-minute encounter with these two beautiful people reminded me that there are blessings always, and that even though we are not in control of events, we are still in control of our attitudes and perspectives. Thank God (literally) for amazing people to come along and remind us of the important things in life.

LESSON #11

CRISES SERVE A PURPOSE

A crisis is an event and truly does nothing to shape you; however, a crisis shows us what we are made of, so to speak—a crisis reveals our true character. If we keep this perspective in our minds, the event is simply that. Even though the event can be devastating (e.g., the death of a spouse), we can look beyond the actual event and work through that event to see the broader picture. There is certainly a need to grieve and a time to be flat on your face in sorrow. These times are vital to our health. I can't imagine not having those personal moments to reflect on Jim and our time together and to be sad over losing him. Jim's illness and death have changed me from who I was prior to the illness. But when I consider the longer-term perspective, I can reflect on better times, on a healthy Jim, on the lessons he shared with me, and our life we had together. I can see him in our children, and I can work to teach the kids Jim's values and my beliefs as a result of working through the crisis. I can help the kids become the people God intended them to be, and there is definite value and joy surrounding that.

A crisis can also serve a valuable purpose in that it reminds us where our priorities are and demands us to re-evaluate our lives. When Jim first became ill, we did question what we were to learn from the experience: Work was being given too high a place in our lives; We had gotten entrenched in the grind and fast pace of our lives; We were not focused enough on God, on our purpose of being here. It is sad that it can take a crisis to make us stop and really consider the things we should be considering on a regular basis. But when a crisis does this and we pause and redirect our efforts for good, then the crisis can be viewed as a blessing in disguise.

No matter how much we want to will away a current or future crisis, it can't happen. We will all face one or more throughout our lifetimes. Crisis will therefore also serve the purpose of testing our faith and growing our faith and dependence on God. That too is a good thing. I have been reminded that God never promises us a life absent of sorrow. In fact, because we live in a fallen world with sin and evil around us, He tells us to expect the opposite. He knows we will have trials, suffering, and will fail many times.

But He also promises to be with us. If we trust God, we will win in the end. This is the greatest promise that keeps a believer going. The ultimate crisis of death becomes the ultimate victory of eternal life.

"For God so loved the world that he gave his one and only Son, that whoever believes in him shall not perish but have eternal life." John 3:16

Blog Entry, October 1, 2014: The Surreal Camping Experience: What the Skies Can Tell Us

We occasionally have experiences that seem so unreal they should be seen in a movie. You know, those stories someone tells you where you think, "yeah, sure, come on . . . " but your friend insists she is telling the truth. Well, I had one of those the other week. My kids and I were at a family camp weekend with our church. I struggled to go on the front end—not because I didn't want to go, but there was so much to do to get prepared physically and there was the mental anguish involved: the ultimate sadness of engaging in these activities without my husband at my side, the reminders of death, unfairness, of being alone. But the three of us went—my eight-year-old son, my five-year-old daughter, and I. It was the right thing to do, and the kids were excited. When we arrived that Friday evening, it was raining cats and dogs, it was dark, the drive took longer than expected, and again, I was thinking I had made a mistake.

But as with most things, once you start, it is fine, and often-times, it is good. The next day brought sunshine, kids playing and laughing, and things felt right. But the skies decided to get cloudy again. The timing was fine as it was mandatory rest time for all campers. Because there was no formal activities available during this time, my kids went scampering off with friends, happy to entertain themselves for the rest period, and I was left alone to return to our cabin. I pulled out the chair and sat on the front porch, admiring the scenery. Our cabin was on the water, there was green grass and trees all around, and I could hear seagulls in the background. And so I sat. The longer I sat and watched, the more I could see, including a man standing on the dock. He wore a blue rain jacket with a hood, and he was alone. I thought that was odd given that up until this time I had never seen a man alone: men were either with their children, their wives, or with other men.

As the clouds continued to roll in, a haze fell over the back-drop of the dock, providing a curtain of darkness behind the man in such a way that I could now see him more clearly. I couldn't figure out what he was doing. It didn't look like any-thing. There was no one else around—rain was inevitable and everyone was indoors. Who was he? The logical part of me said it was a counselor or someone working at the camp, but the longing part of me wanted it to be Jim. Looking away from the man this time, I saw an amazing sight. On the right side of the dock all across the water, the sky and landscape were com-pletely covered with hazy rain. I couldn't make out the hills, the buildings, or anything else. It was a blanket of dew. To the left of the dock, the sky was still visible and the imagery intact. The rain hadn't gotten that far yet.

Two things struck me: 1.) How much more detail I could make out with the haze in place. My attention was directed to the one object I could still see—the man. I could really see him now. I expected Jim to turn around, wave to me, and smile. 2)

How one perspective (mine) could have both cloudy, hazy, dreary on one side and clear, bright on the other. Both are possible at once: there is good present always, even in the sadness.

As I continued to watch the man and the sky, the haze and rain moved across the water. It covered the man eventually, and as the right side of the dock cleared and the left became hazy, things changed once again. As the rain moved on, so too did the man. My Jim was gone when the sun returned to the dock, but I appreciated his reminder to see the clearing through the haze.

ACKNOWLEDGEMENTS

My children, Braxton Young and Annalise Young, have consistently motivated me to give back. They have been a true inspiration to focus my thoughts and to try to provide some meaningful insight to take from this tragedy. Their talents and contributions to the book are most evident. Braxton has a pensive nature about him, taking in much around him and making sense of the world. Annalise has proven to be a great illustrator. I love that both of them have been so enthusiastic about this family project.

Through our many years journey of Jim's illness, death, and now mourning, so many people have provided us with help, love, and support and for all the acts of kindness I am most grateful. We would not have made it as far as we did if it wasn't for all these wonderful people. I am also very appreciative of the enthusiasm for my writings and encouragement that I have received from many of these same people, and for the many strangers who have sent notes or spoken to me after a talk. Such encouragement has given me the push to continue writing.

My editor was Gail Kearns and the book cover and interior designer was Bob Aulicino. Both have been supportive and helpful and the book is much better for their efforts.

ABOUT THE AUTHOR

DR. ERICA KOSAL is a widow, mother, author, speaker, and professor. She lives with her two children in Raleigh, North Carolina. Her passion is to help people find their inner strength and to grow in their resilience and faith. Her first book, *Miracles for Daddy: A Family's Inspirational Fight against a Modern Medical Goliath*, highlights the power of the human spirit through the story focused on Jim's fight with chronic Lyme disease and Erica's resilience and growing faith.

Please visit Erica's website at
http://www.bouncetoresilience.com
and connect with her on facebook under
Miracles For Daddy.

www.ingramcontent.com/pod-product-compliance
Lightning Source LLC
LaVergne TN
LVHW021135080426
835509LV00010B/1358